RAND MᶜNALLY

Primary Atlas

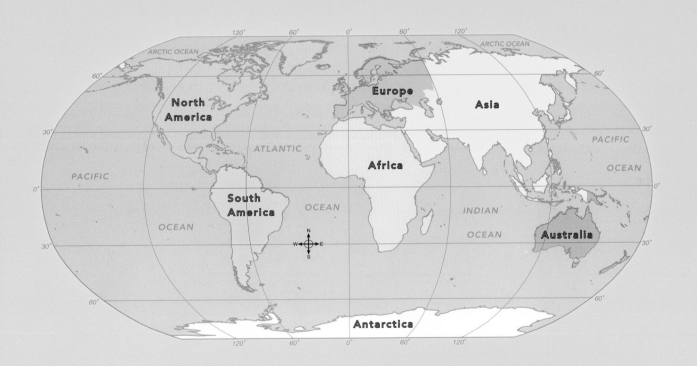

Maps

An **atlas** is a book of maps.
Maps use colors, lines, and shapes to show real places on Earth.
The lines, colors, and shapes are called **symbols**

River

River

Mountains

Mountains

City

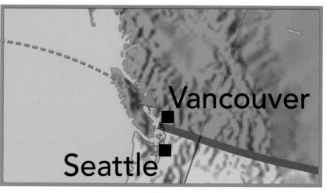

City

A map **legend** tells about symbols.
What symbols do you see in this legend?

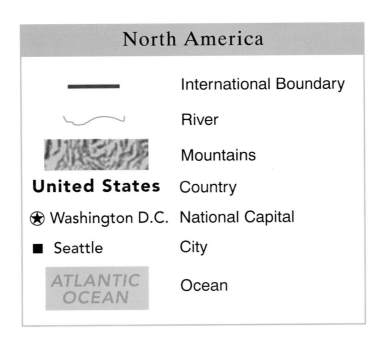

You can find directions on a map.
The **compass rose** shows North, East, South, and West.

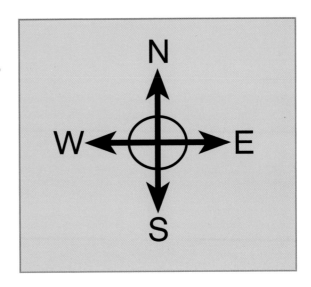

United States

The United States is our country.
Where is your state?

Map Skills

Name a place south of your state.

Mt. Rushmore, South Dakota

Mesa Verde, Colorado

White House, Washington, D.C.

United States

────	International Boundary
────	State Boundary
∿	River
	Mountains
Canada	Country
New Mexico	State
★ Washington D.C.	National Capital
★ Lincoln	State Capital
ATLANTIC OCEAN	Ocean

5

The World

Our world has many countries. The countries are on large land areas called continents.

ARCTIC OCEAN

Greenland
(Denmark)

Russia

Alaska
(United States)

Iceland

Canada

North

America

Ireland

United States

Portugal

ATLANTIC

Moro

Hawaii
(United States)

Cuba

Puerto Rico

Mexico

Mauritani

PACIFIC

Nicaragua

Venezuela

Colombia

South

America

OCEAN

Peru

Brazil

OCEAN

Chile

Argentina

N
W — E
S

The World

——————	International Boundary
∿∿∿	River
▨	Mountains
Asia	Continent
United States	Country
ATLANTIC OCEAN	Ocean

0   1000   2000 Miles

Antarctic Circle

Map Skills

What continent is north of South America?

60°   120°

ARCTIC OCEAN

Sweden   Finland

Russia

Europe   Asia   60°

Poland

Ukraine   Kazakhstan   Mongolia

Italy

Greece   Turkey   China   South   Japan

Iraq   Iran   Korea

Pakistan   30°

Libya   Egypt   Saudi   India   Taiwan   PACIFIC

         Arabia   Oman

ger   Thailand   OCEAN

Chad   Sudan   Yemen   Philippines

eria   Ethiopia

Africa   Malaysia   Equator   0°

abon   Kenya   Indonesia   Papua

Dem. Rep.   New Guinea

of the Congo   Tanzania

Angola   INDIAN

     Zambia

Namibia   Zimbabwe   Madagascar

    Botswana   OCEAN   Australia

South   Australia   30°

Africa

                     New Zealand

                     60°

ntarctica

Copyright by Rand McNally & Co.
Made in U.S.A.
N-PRM10000-P1 -2-1-2

60°   120°

7

North America

North America is the continent where we live.

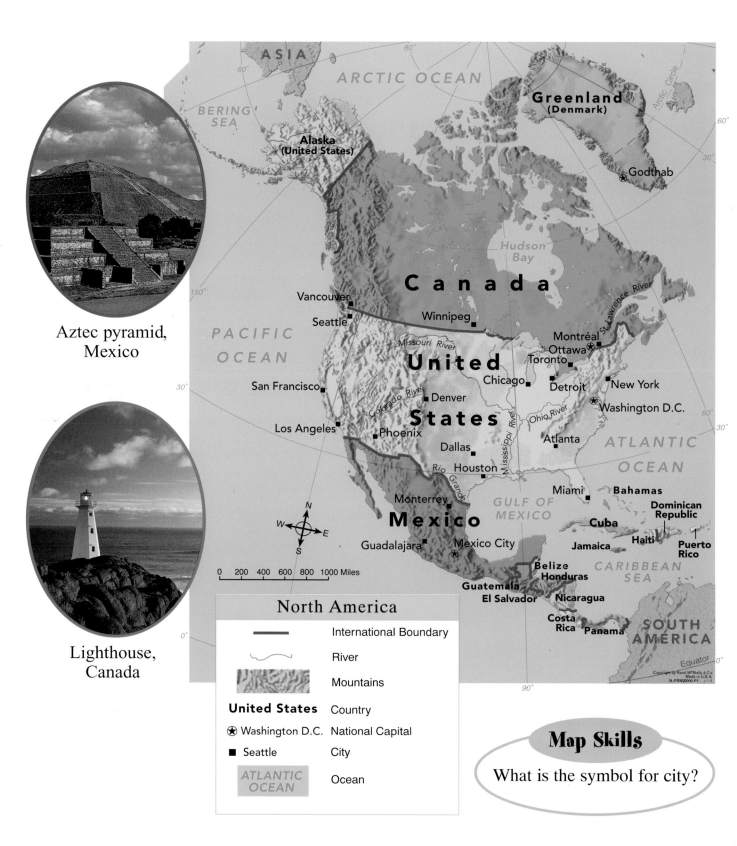

Aztec pyramid, Mexico

Lighthouse, Canada

North America

————	International Boundary
∿	River
(shaded)	Mountains
United States	Country
✪ Washington D.C.	National Capital
■ Seattle	City
ATLANTIC OCEAN	Ocean

Map Skills

What is the symbol for city?

South America

Most of South America is south of the equator.

Rainforest, Brazil

Llamas, Peru

South America

———	International Boundary
∿	River
▨	Mountains
Brazil	Country
✪ Lima	National Capital
■ Sao Paulo	City
ATLANTIC OCEAN	Ocean

Copyright by Rand McNally & Co.
Made in U.S.A.
N-PRM40000-P1

Did you know?

Llamas spit when they get mad!

Europe is a small continent with many countries.

Parthenon, Greece

Eiffel Tower, France

Windmill, Netherlands

Castle, Germany

Map Skills

What is the symbol for national capital?

Europe

——	International Boundary
∿	River
▨	Mountains
Spain	Country
✪ Paris	National Capital
■ Istanbul	City
ATLANTIC OCEAN	Ocean

Did you know?

The person who built the Eiffel Tower helped build the Statue of Liberty.

Asia

Asia is the largest continent.

Panda, China

Taj Mahal, India

EUROPE

Moscow

Rus

Ob

Ankara

Turkey   Georgia

Cyprus   Armenia

Azerbaijan

Lebanon

Israel   Syria

Jerusalem

Jordan   Iraq   Baghdad

Tehran

Kuwait   Iran

Riyadh   Bahrain

Qatar

Saudi   U.A.E.

Arabia

Yemen   Oman

Kazakhstan

Uzbekistan

Turkmenistan

Kyrgyzst

Tajikistan

Afghanistan

Kabul

Islamabad

Pakistan

Karachi   New Delhi   N

Bombay   India

Bangalore   Ma

Sri La

MEDITERRANEAN SEA

AFRICA

RED SEA

CASPIAN SEA

Tigris River

Euphrates River

Ganges

ARABIAN SEA

INDIAN OCEAN

Arctic Circle

60°   80°

AR

30°

30°

60°

Asia

——	International Boundary
〰	River
▨	Mountains
China	Country
✪ Tokyo	National Capital
■ Hong Kong	City
PACIFIC OCEAN	Ocean

N
W   E
S

0   200   400   600   800   1000 Miles

Asia has more people than any other continent.

Did you know?

Pandas often eat 14 hours a day!

Temple, Thailand

Himalaya mountains,
China

Africa

Africa is the warmest continent.

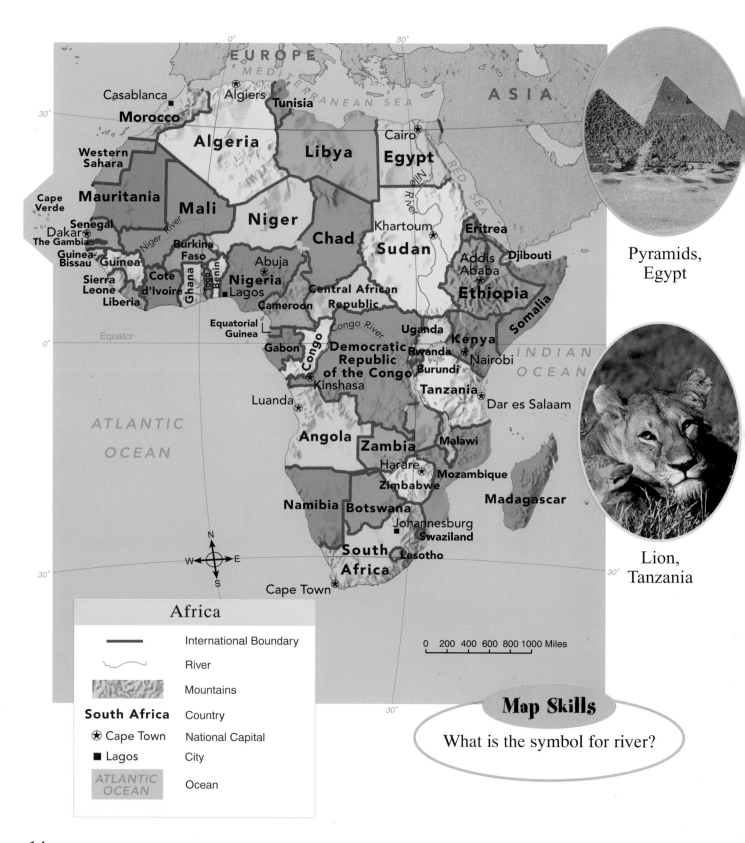

Pyramids,
Egypt

Lion,
Tanzania

Africa

———	International Boundary
∿	River
(texture)	Mountains
South Africa	Country
✪ Cape Town	National Capital
■ Lagos	City
ATLANTIC OCEAN	Ocean

0 200 400 600 800 1000 Miles

Map Skills

What is the symbol for river?